A Call To Love

Second Lesson Sermons
For Sundays After Pentecost
(Middle Third)

Cycle A

Tom M. Garrison

CSS Publishing Company, Inc., Lima, Ohio

A CALL TO LOVE

Copyright © 2001 by
CSS Publishing Company, Inc.
Lima, Ohio

All rights reserved. No part of this publication may be reproduced in any manner whatsoever without the prior permission of the publisher, except in the case of brief quotations embodied in critical articles and reviews. Inquiries should be addressed to: Permissions, CSS Publishing Company, Inc., P.O. Box 4503, Lima, Ohio 45802-4503.

For more information about CSS Publishing Company resources, visit our website at www.csspub.com.

ISBN 0-7880-1830-2   PRINTED IN U.S.A.

*To Renata —
my loving wife — who knows how to speak
to the best in me.*

Acknowledgments

For the love and support of my mother, Audie Garrison, who passed away Epiphany, January 6, 2001.

For my partner in the faith through the years, The Reverend Dr. Gary Carver.

For the Central Christian Church, Uniontown, Pennsylvania, and their continued faith in me and my preaching.

Table Of Contents

Preface   7

Proper 12   9
Pentecost 10
Ordinary Time 17
    Strength Out Of Weakness
    Romans 8:26-39

Proper 13   15
Pentecost 11
Ordinary Time 18
    The Pain Of Caring
    Romans 9:1-5

Proper 14   21
Pentecost 12
Ordinary Time 19
    The Word Of Confession
    Romans 10:5-15

Proper 15   25
Pentecost 13
Ordinary Time 20
    Have Mercy On Me
    Romans 11:1-2a, 29-32

Proper 16   29
Pentecost 14
Ordinary Time 21
    A Living Sacrifice
    Romans 12:1-8

Proper 17   35
Pentecost 15
Ordinary Time 22
    Victims?
    Romans 12:9-21

Proper 18   39
Pentecost 16
Ordinary Time 23
    A Call To Love
    Romans 13:8-14

Proper 19   43
Pentecost 17
Ordinary Time 24
    Who Am I To Judge Another?
    Romans 14:1-12

Proper 20   47
Pentecost 18
Ordinary Time 25
    Living On The Edge
    Philippians 1:21-30

Proper 21   53
Pentecost 19
Ordinary Time 26
    The Mind Of Christ
    Philippians 2:1-13

Lectionary Preaching After Pentecost   59

Preface

It is always with a little reservation that any preacher offers up sermons for public consumption. As with any sermon book, traveling from pulpit to page seems almost like having open house in a prayer chapel. The sermons you will read in this book were preached at Central Christian Church (Disciples of Christ) in Uniontown, Pennsylvania.

I suppose with any preacher the thing most desired is to be heard. That very thought came to me early in my preaching career when I ran across a small book of sermons in an old book store in Chattanooga, Tennessee. The book was *Latimer's Sermons*, which is a collection of seven sermons preached before Edward VI, on each Friday in Lent, 1549. However, what was most interesting about the little book was the desire of Hugh Latimer to be heard. He not only has his sermons recorded, but also a journal of his travels. At one point he gives an interesting little sideline about his travels on May 1, 1538, and says, "Riding home from London, it was my intent to preach in a town on the way, 'because it was a holy day' (Feast of the Apostles Philip and James). Expected to find a great company in the church, but was forced to give way to Robin Hood." As one reads his statements following, it is very easy to tell that he was quite insulted that the people went to hear Robin Hood rather than the good Bishop.

I feel some kinship to Bishop Latimer when it comes to being heard. If there is anything that we desire as preachers, it is not so much to be gifted, but rather to be heard. I hope that in listening to these sermons each person will find something that will be useful.

A few months ago I made a trip to San Miguel de Allende, Mexico, a wonderful little town built by the Spaniards in the sixteenth century. One morning I walked up to the maitre d' of a beautiful outdoor restaurant and asked him if I might have a specific table with a splendid view. He said, "Senor, this is your home." I came to find out this meant just what it said: "While you are here ... this is yours ... use it like your home." It is my desire that those who read this book might make it theirs. Take time to walk with me in the pulpit and then, on the other hand, sit with my congregation as you listen to these sermons. If you can hear my words and let some of them be a source of inspiration in preaching, teaching, or even in lifting the heart just a bit, then, these sermons are well worth the paper they are written on.

Proper 12
Pentecost 10
Ordinary Time 17
Romans 8:26-39

Strength Out Of Weakness

It was the July 22, 1999, CNN live coverage of the burial at sea of John F. Kennedy, Jr. All his family members were dressed in black, knowing that in a few minutes the remains of someone they loved would be forever committed to the sea. When the coverage from the first news of the plane crash began to air — one of the main subjects was all the tragedy that this family has suffered, beginning with the little boy the press called John-John, standing with a salute for his fallen father, the President of the United States. As those visions passed across the television screen, the sound of the horses with the caissons still pulled at the heart strings. The next scene was that of Robert Kennedy lying on a kitchen floor of a hotel in Los Angeles after winning the state in the 1968 presidential campaign. The tragedies seem almost endless as the remaining head of the family, Ted Kennedy, stood with Caroline doing the unthinkable: taking the ashes of America's young prince and committing them back to the waters that took his life. The American dream shattered over and over again for this family, leaving nothing but suffering. Yet somehow in all this is the realization that there will be strength to guide them through their weakness.

Weakness — what a strange word. We all know we have it. In fact, the one thing we do not like to admit or to show is our weakness.

Weakness — something we do not teach our children about because it is our desire for them to be self-reliant.

Weakness — something we will correct if at all possible.

It is after the open heart surgery and the doctor comes into the room. You expect the words: "Rest, take your time, and it will heal." However, the very thing that will make it heal is the thing that will overcome the weakness: exercise. How in the world do you overcome this weakness? The only answer is with strength.

Weakness — sometimes it is that very thing that we learn to depend on.

As I opened the door to her hospital room the last time I visited her, Lou looked at me as she took the last drag of her cigarette and said, "Well, the doctor came in and told me I could have a cigarette." I took her hand as she continued in a very low, raspy voice, "If there is one weakness I have, this is it. I've tried to quit but I can't, and now it's too late. I thought it was my strength but it is my weakness."

In today's text the Apostle Paul focuses for a moment on some kind of weakness. It may not be a deadly habit, a recovery from open heart surgery, or a family broken by grief. It may be that the weakness Paul stops for a moment to talk about is the weakness we all suffer and endure. It is difficult to imagine that Paul would even bring up this subject of weakness. For him to say, "The Spirit helps us in our weakness," is like Tiger Woods signing up for golf lessons. Of all people, it would seem Paul is most unlikely to be short on understanding God and knowing how our spirit connects with God's Spirit.

That is why it seems strange for Paul, above all, to admit any kind of weakness. In any situation he is a hero to all those who have studied him. At what point does Paul's weakness arise? Is it in the pulpit? It does not seem so, even though some of the Corinthians thought preaching was not his greatest gift. He would stand in Athens and speak to people who did not understand the concept of one God. Paul preached: "In him we live and move and have our being; as even some of your poets have said, 'For we are indeed his offspring.' "

Of all things, Paul doesn't have weakness when it comes to his preaching. In fact, he boldly prays, "I thank my God in all my remembrance of you, always in every prayer of mine for you all making my prayer with joy, thankful for your partnership in the gospel from the first day until now" (Philippians 1:3-5). Even when he is writing from prison and threatened with death he says, "To live is Christ and to die is gain." Where is the weakness of Paul?

These words are for us also when we think our strength is in ourselves. Maybe that is why Paul makes the statement: "The Spirit helps us in our weakness." The only question that comes is: How does that happen?

The Spirit speaks to God when we pray about things we cannot even imagine ourselves coming to God with. The Spirit is the ally of our soul that guides us down roads that are not traveled very often. Some lines from the Robert Frost poem, "The Road Not Taken," puts our weakness and strength into the proper perspective.

Two roads diverged in a wood, and I —
I took the one less traveled by,
And that has made all the difference.

The strength we are talking about is something that God does for us, through the Spirit, which we are not capable of doing for ourselves. It is becoming and being something that we never thought we could be. It is facing and going through situations that would seem impossible to our hearts and souls. How often do we see someone whose life has been lifted to a higher level when it looked like all that was there was weakness? A prayer or a hope was the only thing that the individual could cling to, and even with that there wasn't any confidence that those things would work.

My great aunt used to say, "You never see people until you see them in their true weakness." Maybe that is what Paul is saying — it is not until we face the things that take the breath out of our lungs that we can really breathe the Spirit of life. Some of this I know by Paul's writing, but most of it I know because of what I have observed in the weakness and helplessness of those to whom I have ministered. As I thought of this fact there is one story that keeps bringing itself to my mind. It is shared out of pain that reminds me of where strength appears and lives.

It was the Saturday before Mother's Day and I was out of town when my secretary called to tell me one of our college students had been killed. Rob had just finished his first year at Texas Christian University and was about to drive home to Tennessee the next day. On Friday he had gone to a tire store to have everything checked out before his road trip. During the wait he was on the phone with his mom. While he was talking, a man came into the store with the intent of robbery. He hung up the phone for Rob and ushered him and the store manager to the back room. Rob thought he could take him, since he had been a good wrestler in school. The store manager heard two shots; one went into the ceiling and the other went into Rob's back. He died in the arms of the store manager.

That Sunday morning the local paper carried the headlines in bold letters "Happy Mother's Day" and almost directly under it a large picture of Rob slain two days before. I am not sure how a family gets through such a period of devastation or weakness. But I know that somehow, with the Spirit's help, something happens.

The January following that event the U.S. was at war with Iraq. We as a nation were holding our breath, and when we were breathing, it was in prayer. The church I was serving also paused a number of times to pray. In preparation for one of those occasions, we announced that we would have a special prayer service. It would not only be for the end of Desert Storm, but for any other need that arose. I knew that Rob's mother would be traveling to Texas the next morning to witness the trial of Rob's murderer. She came to me at the end of the service and said, "The prayer service is Wednesday night?" My response was, "I know you will be needing some special prayers and we will lift you and your family in our prayers." She thanked me. But the thing she seemed concerned about was what she did next. She placed a small piece of paper into my hand. As I looked at the paper with just a name on it, she said, "Please have the church pray for him." My response was, "Of course, we will. But who is this?" She again said, "Please have the church pray for him." I said, "I will, but who is it?" Finally with a long sigh, she said, "It is the man that killed my Rob."

Some things can come only when the Spirit takes over and somehow we become what we never thought we could be, because the Spirit himself intercedes for us with sighs too deep for words. There are occasions when those sighs come to the surface and we know that God has taken our hearts to places we did not know could exist.

Through this passage the one underlying statement that brings strength through the weakness must be Paul's wondrous line that continues to speak to us: "We know that all things work together for good for those who love God, who are called according to his purpose."

How is it that in this weakness all things work together for good? The only way is to let our weakness be put into the hands of the one who supplies strength from places we cannot discover on our own. It is now the time to open ourselves to the power that appears to be weakness, just as God chose to come in the form of a baby, without strength. And that baby became a man whose strength the world would come to know by the cross. Paul closes this section with a quote from Psalms. He emphatically says: "No, in all these things we are more than conquerors through him who loved us." Therefore, the horizon expands dramatically. It is here we as people of God are able to look into the face of a power greater than ourselves and know the strength available. God's strength is ours and the advantage still belongs to those who have learned the important lessons of the heart.

In the movie about the famed Presbyterian preacher Peter Marshall, as he is being taken to the hospital the last time, he looks at his wife Catherine and says, without reservation, "I will see you in the morning." Faith upon faith and strength out of our weakness.

**Proper 13
Pentecost 11
Ordinary Time 18
Romans 9:1-5**

The Pain Of Caring

Amazing statements have a powerful way of burning themselves into our memories. Examples of this are statements that are filled with care. I recall the cry of the Reverend Dr. Martin Luther King, Jr., as he stood at the Lincoln Memorial: "I have a dream...." And as he preached that sermon, it seemed that everyone knew the problem. It wasn't about race or rights, it was about getting a nation to care about all her people.

When you feel that you are neglected or mistreated, you feel that no one cares. The act of truly caring transcends the problems of race and rights. Caring may be the one commodity that can transform a person's being and behavior. It has the most powerful motivation. It will send nations to war. It will cause men and women to give their greatest gifts for that care to be accomplished.

I recall hearing Dr. Fred Craddock preach a sermon about caring. One of the things he pointed out was that the seven deadly sins, the list of mortal sins during the Middle Ages, began with "sloth," This first sin had its root in the meaning "I don't care." For example, you see an old woman pushing a shopping basket with all her worldly goods inside, and your response is, "Well, she's not my mother." Or you see a starving child with a distended belly, begging for food, and your response is, "Well, he isn't my child."

The most painful thing for a person to know is that he or she is not cared for. There is, however, another pain that can cut just as deep. It doesn't have to do with someone caring for us. It has to do with us caring for someone else.

It is painful when someone has accused you of being uncaring. One of the greatest insults to anyone would be that they had no care or concern for those closest to them. It seems that Paul has been accused of not really caring for his own people. Paul is being hurt by someone or some church, and to defend himself he rises up with the most emotional statements of his career. Listen to Paul in this passage. Listen to him defending himself. Feel the words coming from the depth of his heart. He says: "I am speaking the truth in Christ. I am not lying. I have great sorrow and unceasing anguish in my heart. For I wish I were accursed ... for my people." Paul must somehow convince the people that he does care. I can only imagine from this statement the pain Paul must have been suffering because of his care. It would hurt anyone to think that others thought one indifferent. Maybe the hurt comes from knowing how much pain exists with people who are not cared for.

It hurt to know the story of the seventeen-year-old teenager who was taken to the hospital for emergency surgery. As he was being prepped, his father was called to come to the hospital. His sister stood at the desk as their father carefully looked over the forms. Then he asked the clerk, "Does this mean I will have to pay for this?" "Why, yes," the clerk said.

The father then slid the papers back to her and said, "I will not sign." After the surgery, and upon discharge from the hospital, the young man was all alone. They had him sign a number of papers so the hospital could collect from other agencies. As he sat there with pen in hand, the lady behind the desk finally said, "You are like a man without a country."

The famed movie about World War II, *Saving Private Ryan*, brings us to know how the feelings remain after years. The story line involves a family that has lost four of their five sons to the war. The War Department decides that it is enough. A squad is sent through Europe to find one private to send him home. Soldiers lose their lives in order to find Private Ryan. Finally, the movie reaches its climax fifty years later with a now-old man crying, asking if he is a good person. He wants to be sure that his life has been worth what was given for it. It is a scene that reaches into the heart and examines if we all have cared enough.

The Apostle Paul seems tormented by this word that has come to him concerning some indifference. This word was coming from his own people, those that were the chosen nation. It may have seemed to them that Paul, a very zealous Jew, was uncaring and had turned his back on his kinsmen. It would look that way to those who believed their God was the God of Israel. When he became a follower of Jesus the Christ, it would seem as though Paul had ripped the Star of David off his chest and thrown it into the dirt. It would appear that Paul had disregarded everything about his heritage. However, the problem was not only the acceptance of Jesus Christ as Savior, but also the inclusion of those who were not in the scheme of things as the Jewish people saw it. For Paul to accept the non-Jew was for him to say, "I care nothing about my own people." So Paul responds to these accusations by expressing his most heartfelt pain. It hurt to the bottom of his heart to hear someone say to him, "You do not care for us."

Paul's agony over these accusations is so great that he makes a dramatic statement in his desire to convince his critics of his heartfelt care. He says, "For I could wish that I myself were accursed and cut off from Christ for the sake of my brethren, my kinsmen by race" (v. 3). That statement is a statement not only of self-sacrifice but of eternal separation for the sake of others. Paul, of all people, knew what it would mean to be cut off.

I recall the story of an ancient oriental king who met with his counselors to make a decision about a recurring crime that was being committed. They decided that the punishment should serve both as a punishment, as well as an example. The pronouncement was made that the next person caught in the commission of this crime would lose the sight in two eyes. A sharp iron rod, heated until cherry red, would be touched to each eye. The result would be immediate, the deepest darkness for the longest day one would live on earth. There would be no exception to the decree. Noble or servant would receive the same punishment. It was performed several times after perpetrators came before the king. Then, another was apprehended in the commission of this particular crime. He was arrested, taken to the royal prison, and awaited his audience with the king. As the criminal was taken before the king, he lifted his head. It was the king's own son. The king thought, "How can I take the sight from my own son?" He called his counselors and they read and reread the law. There could be no exception. The punishment for the crime would be the loss of sight in two eyes. The king, bewildered, asked, "Is not the punishment for this crime the loss of sight in two eyes?" The counselors responded, "Yes, that satisfies judgment and meets the condition of the law that has been passed." The king looked at his son and said, "Take one of mine and one of my son's." So they did.

Paul said if there was some way possible he could show his people his care, he would give himself in a fashion that would be the greatest sacrifice. He said, "I am telling the truth. I am not lying; my conscience bears me witness in the Holy Spirit."

The greatest gift Paul could show to others was simply to express his care; a care that was made of sacrifice, a care that was not a pat on the back or simply a smile. It was a care that went to the very heart of the gospel and sacrifice. The very central element of the gospel is the fact that there is one that came to humankind to demonstrate the care of God. He came to live and teach, but much more than that. He came not only to express the heartfelt concern, but also finally to lay down a life that would serve as a sacrifice for so many others. Paul's statement was more than a statement of care; it was a messianic statement of caring so much as to sacrifice his very self.

Somehow we know the greatness of this sacrifice, but at the same time we have the idea that our care is only for the ones we love. Paul was reminded of God's care for those that did not seem worthy. Jesus, himself, said, "God makes the rain fall on the good and the bad, and the sun shine on the righteous and unrighteous." It seems to mean that God does not have two standards of conduct or behavior. God does not allow God's love to be governed by other people. That is, God is not bad to bad people and good to good people. But we humans find it easy to be nice to nice people and mean to mean people. We only care about people that care about us.

The drawback to this is: "Who is determining one's behavior?" Nice people make one nice, and mean people make one mean. These two groups of people are determining one's behavior. How can God remain impartial and unbiased? It is simply that God does not react, but acts out of God's own self.

Now we are able to see the problem of caring. We are to behave toward others according to our own character, according to our own love, and not according to the way other people may or may not act. To be impartial one must act out of one's own impartial love.

Human beings are constantly searching for someone who really, really cares. When all is said and done if only there is care, it will be enough. "You are like a man without a country." The words the lady at the hospital desk spoke still haunt the man some thirty years later. The thing that comes back from that episode in his life is the fact that there should have been someone who cared about him and not about the cost, and that his own flesh and blood was unwilling to assume the bill. A father should have, deep inside, a care for a son. The pain that is felt when someone one knows should care and does not, can only be felt in the same measure by those who truly care yet who know others think they do not.

Paul finally said in his attempt to express his heart: "You want to know how much I really care about my own people? Or how much I am willing to do for my own people? You put me here as a teacher of the gospel and lover of humankind, and then you put my kinspeople across the gulf — those that are in need of what I teach. Then you put hell between us. I would give myself, if I could only know my people could come to God through Jesus Christ. That is my pain of caring." A pain we all share.

**Proper 14
Pentecost 12
Ordinary Time 19
Romans 10:5-15**

The Word Of Confession

On January 21, 2001, George W. Bush was sworn in as the forty-third President of the United States. As I sat and watched the events of the day, I thought what it meant for our new President, what it meant for our nation, and what it meant to the world. As he gave the inaugural speech, he lifted up the ideas of character and commitment. He quoted Mother Teresa and referred to the story Jesus told about the Good Samaritan. All in all, he said the same things that presidents before him have said, and the media spent hours upon hours laboriously interpreting his words.

The President's speech was another example of what it means to speak a word, or to take an oath, thereby giving one's word. It marked the significance of a word, and how words can and will affect lives. Maybe that is why a great deal of Paul's writing deals with words and how they affect our salvation. Paul shows in Romans chapter 10 that God, in God's total and unfettered freedom, has chosen to make his grace, his care, and his forgiveness available to everyone. How does this transaction take place? How do all people have access to the grace of God? Paul answers, "By the Word. By the Word of faith which we preach!" This word is near us, in our mouths, and in our hearts. If you confess with your mouth, "Jesus is Lord," and "God raised him from the dead," you will be saved. That which you believe in your heart, you will confess with your lips.

This confession is the word of faith. It is the word that is preached. It is the word that is heard. It is the Word of God. This is the means God *uses* to establish faith everywhere. Some people find it very surprising that at the center of God's grand scheme of redemption for the world is the fragile experience that we call the speaking and hearing of a word — that fragile movement of vibrations across the eardrum. After all, it is just a word. Maybe that is why we should say a word about a word.

As we consider the transaction that Paul is suggesting, we should recall Jesus' words in Matthew 12:36-37: "I tell you, on the day of judgment men will render account for every careless word they utter; for by your words you will be justified, and by your words you will be condemned."

Jesus is pointing out that a person speaks out of the heart. Speaking is that revelation of whom and what we are. So he slides every word to the eternal accountability. Therefore, by our speaking we will be held eternally accountable; by our speaking we will be justified; by our speaking we will be condemned.

It somehow surprises us that Jesus would put so much weight on a word, and that Paul has put at the heart of the transaction of salvation a word. We know that words are just words and anybody can talk. Anyone in the world can say words, and it really isn't all that important these things that we speak. I remember talking to a judge about his time on the bench. He made a remarkable statement — it surprised me, but yet it didn't surprise me. He said that more lies are told on the witness stand than anywhere else in the world. It is that place that you're asked to raise your right hand and swear to tell the truth, the whole truth, and nothing but the truth.

There is a philosophy that says, "We want deeds not words — words don't mean anything." It is the old children's idea about words. I remember this from the time I was very young. We would be called names by the other children and then we would say our little ditty: "Sticks and stones may break my bones, but words will never harm me."

It sounds great and it is a marvelous saying, however, there is one thing wrong with it. It is false. Sticks and stones may break my bones, but words will totally destroy me. I recently visited a woman who was about to celebrate her 105th birthday. She is still alert and has a great sense of humor. However, when we sat and talked about her life, she became sad and told me a story about her life as a little girl. As she told the story, I could sense that her memory went all the way back to the age of eight or nine. She then looked at me and said, "Let me tell you what my daddy said to me." He had been very strict and harsh to her as a child, and this woman now 105 years old had never ever forgotten those words. How is it that we feel words do not mean anything when they reside inside us for as long as we live?

These things called words are events in the realm of sound, but it is our way to relate to each other and to God. And we in churches should give great care to the words we are charged with keeping. We are somehow careless with words, and it is the idea if we say a lot of words that we are performing our job. I have a very good friend who is a member of another denomination. Their senior pastor retired, and in the process of looking for another pastor an interim was hired. My friend asked what I thought about a subject that he felt was inappropriate that had been discussed in the sermon the week before. It was words, only words, but they were words that he knew, and we all know, can and will have an effect on our thinking and on our lives. Our responsibility is not just for the care of souls but for the care of words.

The vocabulary of the faith is extremely important. It is where our hearts, minds, and souls learn their language. Maybe as Christians we should never say something is just a word. It is the importance that Paul found in his letter and the gospel that could only be transmitted with a word. I learned the importance of a word to a mother who had lost her son in the Vietnam War. He was shot down in 1971. Elsie's home was a shrine to her son. She showed me pictures and then she brought out a cassette tape of his voice. He had mailed it the week before he died. She hung on every word of it as if she was hearing it for the first time. I listened to the tape, which was now ten years old. And as he came to the end, he said, "Mom, I love you." Just words, but the tears were flowing down her cheeks just the same.

Have you ever thought about what it is you do when you say a word? To speak is to create a whole new experience for someone. As we visit the nursing home or the hospital, it amazes me what a word can do. On one occasion I recall walking into a personal care home, searching for an elderly gentleman. We found him in a day room with about eight other people. As we walked in, our saying good morning changed the complexion of the room. For people we don't even know, words can have the effect of turning on a light or encouraging them to sit up straight. It is only a word.

A word is a powerful, powerful thing. It was the night Jesus would be betrayed and he would prepare for the drama before him as the Savior of the world. It was during the Passover meal that Jesus took the bread, blessed it, broke it, and gave it to the disciples saying, "Take, eat, this is my body." Then, after supper he took the cup, blessing it and giving it to his disciples, saying, "All of you drink of this cup. It is the blood for the remission of sins." What Jesus did that night was to take a supper and make a sacrament. He did this simply by speaking a word. When you say something, you may be creating a new world or a new experience for someone.

The Apostle Paul calls on believers to understand the power of this word called confession. And the prominent theme from the early chapters of Romans returns as Paul recalls that God's salvation knows no boundaries. He expresses that God is "Lord of All" and generous to all, and everyone who calls on God will be saved. God calls us to have a faith that will act on word and deed. I believe that statement contains the raw material that can change a church, a family, and the world.

When you say a word, you break someone's silence. You throw a stone against the clear glass of silence and interrupt their world with your love. It is this word that leads to a word of salvation. We are justified by words, and yet the most difficult thing in the world to do is to have a meaningful conversation. Because, as we speak about things that are so deep inside, the first thing to go is our voice. It is difficult to speak the most profound things in the world. This may be why, in our tradition after pastor's class has been completed and Palm Sunday and Easter approach, we know those being baptized will make a confession. The confession is never one that is shouted, but it is spoken from the deep places of the heart. Those are the things God calls us to — things that we look for the most — the places that sit at the bottom of our heart.

Proper 15
Pentecost 13
Ordinary Time 20
Romans 11:1-2a, 29-32

Have Mercy On Me

"Lord, have mercy on me." My earliest memory of that statement goes back to a little farm in central Alabama. It was summertime. That meant I would be spending about two weeks with my Aunt Etta and Uncle Lee near Fayette. One of my favorite times was when I would hear in the distance that familiar rumble of the mail truck. I ran to meet the mailman as fast as my feet would carry me. I could hardly wait to give the letter to Aunt Etta, because without doubt she would say, "Lord, have mercy on me" if she received a letter from her sister, my grandmother.

I thought it was an old term because it seemed to me that old people were the only ones who used the term: people like Sam, the old black man who came to help out around our little farm. Whenever there was a reason for any type of amazement, the words Sam always said were, "Have mercy on my soul."

I wondered what the word *mercy* meant. Have *mercy* on me! Have *mercy* on my soul!

"Your Honor, my client knows that what he did was damaging to the families involved, to the community, to his own family, and even to himself. He would like to throw himself on the *mercy* of this court."

In the temple — in the Holy of Holies — the Ark of the Covenant sat. The mercy seat flanked by two cherubim was on top of the Ark. It was there that once a year the high priest would sprinkle blood from a lamb to atone for the sins of the people.

Mercy: Jesus told a story about two men who went to the temple to pray. One felt very self-righteous. He prayed loudly, thanking

God that he was not like other people. He was filled with an attitude of superiority as he prayed. The other man who came to the temple to pray would not even lift his eyes toward heaven. He prayed to God saying, "Lord, forgive me a sinner. Lord, have mercy on me."

I wondered and so I asked Aunt Etta one day after she got one of those long-awaited letters. "What does it mean? These words you say: 'Have mercy on me'?"

"Well, let me see," she began, "that word mercy means God doing something good for you." All that summer I walked around saying, "Have mercy on me," but somehow it didn't really feel the same as when I heard older people say it. So I just thought about it.

But I have come to learn that she was right. I learned that grace is the unmerited favor of God. Grace is getting something you do not deserve. I learned that justice is the dreaded sentence of getting what you deserve. And, mercy is that gift of not getting what you deserve. In other words, "God is doing something good for you."

I remember Dr. Rex Turner when I was first taking religion classes. One day he opened his class with an unusual question. "Which would you rather have from God, justice or mercy?" This was his way of opening up dialogue in the area of what it means for God to be merciful, as well as what it means for us to be merciful.

Paul makes the statement that God is merciful to all people — *to all people*. One of the most difficult concepts for us to understand is God's choice to be merciful to all people. I want God to be merciful to all *good* people in life.

I recently watched a program on *A & E* about Death Row inmates. They were waiting to be put to death. In our hearts we say, "Give them what they deserve. They killed. They raped. They should get what they deserve. The courts have said they should be put to death, so put them to death." Paul says that God will be merciful to people even if they have committed some of the most heinous crimes imaginable. You see, this word mercy means you don't get what you deserve.

On a lesser scale — imagine the scenario that you have been going to church with him for 35 years, and five years ago you stopped speaking. It was in a board meeting that the voices got loud, the faces got red, and the hands got shaky. Things were said that shouldn't have been said, in a way that shouldn't have been expressed. How do you come together and pray, sing, and celebrate? It seems there is only one way for reconciliation and peace. There is only one way, and that one way is mercy.

Giving mercy isn't the easiest thing to do. For when you do it, it seems like you just go along with the wrong. Whenever there is a decision by a jury or a judge that seems full of mercy, the feeling that comes is that they have aligned themselves with the crime. The comment comes very quickly. "I can't believe that judge would just go along with that sort of thing."

Or imagine this scene:

"Albert, what are you doing?"

"Well, Mother, I'm moving back home."

"Son, I know you are 45, but why would you do that? Have you been seeing Shirley?"

"Yes, Mother, I have."

"Well, do I need to remind you what she did?"

"Mother, I'm going back."

"If it were me, I would give her exactly what she deserves and that is nothing. She would not get the house, the cars, and especially the children."

"Mother, you don't understand. I have forgiven her."

"Of all things, I can't believe my only son would go along with a thing like she has done. How can you condone actions like these?"

You see, when you put mercy into life and let it work, it looks very much like we are just going along.

Paul said, "Look at life this way: just as you have received mercy, they have received mercy." Maybe the reason it seems so hard is because we not only want to be treated well, we do not want other people to be treated better than we think they should be. This seems to be the major point of the parable Jesus told as recorded in Matthew 20:1-20. It is a story of a man who goes to the market early in the morning and hires workers and agrees on what the wage should be. He returns to hire more at 9 a.m., noon, 3 p.m., and 5 p.m. However, when the day is done at 6 p.m., he pays them all the same starting from the ones that were hired last. This causes a great deal of dissatisfaction to the ones who were hired first, for they thought the others were overcompensated. The act of mercy often causes that type of feeling that we are overcompensating people. They are people that everyone knows, including God, do not deserve what they are getting.

When we come down to the bottom line of our hearts, we know it is true. Mercy is giving to all these people what they do not deserve. The only thing is that the people we are talking about is *us*. We, most of all, need this wonderful little word, mercy. Aunt Etta was right. Mercy is God doing something good for you. May God have mercy on us.

Proper 16
Pentecost 14
Ordinary Time 21
Romans 12:1-8

A Living Sacrifice

I had always assumed I understood the word "sacrifice." A recent trip to Mexico City, however, washed away any ideas I previously held. I had gone through life with the biblical language firmly fixed in my mind. I knew that Paul said, "Present your bodies as a living sacrifice." That does not even come close to what I experienced. On my first day of touring Mexico City with Roberto, he began to give me the history of the city, and the 300-year journey the Aztec Indians made to find the place of the eagle and the snake. We walked past the hall of the conquerors to an excavated sight of ruins that dated back to the fourteenth century. As I walked through the museum, I was amazed by the understanding that these Aztec Indians had of the relationship between their gods and human life. One depiction was of the leaders of their people, the chief priest, and the ruler standing atop one of the larger pyramids. Down the face of the pyramids ran the blood of those who had been sacrificed. The blood was a trademark of the total dedication of these people, with the possible exception of those who had been sacrificed. It seemed that these sacrifices were so much a part of the culture that there were those who would face sacrifice from the time of their birth. To sacrifice and to be sacrificed was a way to satisfy the gods. This rite of offering was performed for hundreds of years. It was not only part of the ritual, it was part of life.

A few hundred feet away from the museum was a Catholic cathedral. I suddenly became aware as I walked inside this massive church built out of the Aztec pyramids that there was another image of sacrifice. This one was a large crucifix above the altar. It was that sacrifice that put into focus the sacrifices that had been performed virtually on that spot. As I went away from downtown Mexico City, a keener understanding of Paul's words existed in my heart.

It is with these images of sacrifice that we move to the writing of the Apostle Paul and the sacrifice he challenges us to become. The section of scripture Paul writes here is a movement away from the theological understanding of the Christian faith. It is a movement toward practical Christian living: what it means to live under the Lordship of Jesus Christ. The Apostle says here that the clearest image he wishes to use as the description of a Christian life is the act of sacrifice, the presenting of life to God. This is a very lofty view of human life. Most of us think of ourselves as being too low, too wicked, too wrong, or too unworthy. Paul pauses and emphasizes our gifts to God as being able to give our best. Then he pauses again, and writes, "I bid you not to think more highly of yourself than you ought to think." Notice, he doesn't say what that is, or how high we ought to think of ourselves. Paul seems to be saying not to think of ourselves more highly than we ought to think, but at the same time, to think of ourselves as gifted. The way the whole church will benefit is to let everyone exercise his or her gift.

Yet how in the world can we offer ourselves as a spiritual sacrifice if we do not understand the gifts we offer? In order to appreciate the gifts fully there must be an understanding of our opinion of ourselves. In our culture we talk about self-image and self-confidence. Paul says we are to think of ourselves as gifted. There seem to be three avenues to travel in response to self-image. One is pride, thinking too highly of ourselves. The second avenue is low self-esteem, thinking less than we should of ourselves. The last avenue is a healthy self-image, being able to offer ourselves to God as the right kind of sacrifice.

If we take time to look at two of the three, we will find that they are deadly and will bring personal and spiritual harm. The pride or arrogance in self or religion is hurtful not only to us but to others. Most of the problems that Jesus dealt with had to do with religious arrogance. When he encountered the Pharisees, the questions were not of the well-being of another person, but some law that may have been broken. Jesus' healing of a man recorded in John 5 is a wonderful example of this. The man had been sick 38 years and Jesus told the man to take up his bed and walk. The man was healed, however, on the sabbath. The Pharisees condemned him for carrying his bed and had no concern for his health or wellbeing. The problem was that they were spiritually arrogant. When Jesus was with people on the outside of Jewish purity, these religious people complained that he was eating with sinners. Jesus replied that he came to save sinners and not to save the saved. This attitude is not found only in Jesus' day. Not only have I known people who have expressed a superior attitude, but I was brought up in a tradition that proudly expressed it.

It was a group who professed to have perfect and complete knowledge of the truth, and who looked with disdain on anyone who was different or believed differently. To claim to speak only absolute truth is to be self-deceived, guilty of both arrogance and foolishness. This problem is a very real problem, and Paul's words here would certainly be a big help. Do not think of yourselves more highly than you ought. But do think of yourselves as gifted. These words, "Don't think of yourselves more highly than you ought," are ringing words, but Paul doesn't say how high that is. I find Paul's expression here of a living sacrifice in great contrast with what a *few* Christians do. Many people have been so afraid of the characteristic of Pride that they have run to the other extreme and joined in the massive put-down in our society.

A survey taken of high school students asked, "What is the worst thing that can happen to you?" The number one answer was: "to be put down in front of my friends." The illiteracy rate in my part of the country is alarmingly high. A friend involved in adult education says the number one problem of educating adults who have limited formal education is the embarrassment factor or the fear that someone might make light of their condition.

Being put down or embarrassed continues to drive the self-image to an unhealthy level. It was just a few days ago that I had to make a trip to a government office. As I walked into the crowded waiting room, there was a sign beside the desk which read: "Take a number. DO NOT COME TO THE DESK BEFORE YOUR

NUMBER IS CALLED." While waiting, I watched the people before me take a legal length sheet of paper and struggle to fill it out only to be reprimanded when the form wasn't filled out properly. Finally one elderly lady trying for the third time told the lady behind the desk, "I don't need what you offer so badly as to be treated this way," and she walked out. People will do without necessities rather than be put down.

A fifty-year-old man I know does not have a relationship with his father because his father finds some way to put him down every time they are around each other. So he and his siblings stay away from their father as much as possible. The man says it would be quite different if his father had gotten this way as he got older, but the father has put his children down since they were young.

During the process of life those things that build you up and those things that put you down will stay with you for a lifetime. Entertainer Jerry Lewis was talking about his career in an interview. After he became famous, he was invited back to his hometown and to the school he attended. He said that in the sixth grade he was put back, and the way the school did it was degrading. He said when he went back for his day of celebration, he requested a meeting with the school board to talk about how children are held back. He expressed the way he felt degraded and from that day forward they changed the procedure. He said that was the good part, then very quietly said, "You know, it still hurts. It still hurts."

We seem to get on this thing about humility. What it means for many is to stand and count our shoelaces. We are so afraid that someone will think too highly of himself or herself that we need to keep them humble. In fact, we have an expression that equates being a human being with making a mistake or being weak. Almost everyone knows the expression, "After all, I'm only human." When Grandma burns the blackberry pie and it tastes like tar, she says, "Well, I'm only human." Then she makes her lemon pie so beautifully and delicious. It tastes like the sun just came up. What is she then?

Paul says we are called to offer a sacrifice of ourselves, and that sacrifice is the best that can be offered. To offer the gifts that are the best is what is expected, and there isn't one person who isn't gifted. We come with an array of gifts. Paul says, "Having gifts that differ according to the grace given to us, let us use them."

Maybe it is time to appreciate the supreme sacrifice given for us and allow ourselves to have a healthy attitude and disposition in the sacrifice we give to God. After all, we are the crowns of God's creation. We are created in God's image and priceless in God's sight. Every one of us has something to give to humankind and to God.

**Proper 17
Pentecost 15
Ordinary Time 22
Romans 12:9-21**

Victims?

After watching *Gandhi*, the acclaimed movie about the non-violent leader of India, for the sixth time, I felt what I had felt at every previous viewing. "Did this man lead a life of being a victim or a victor?" He allowed himself to be imprisoned and to starve as a weapon against the British Empire. He somehow mobilized a nation through a non-violent force. He lived a very simple life, and it did not make sense to the British Empire that one could become victorious by being what seemed to everyone a victim.

That is the way I feel when I read the Bible. Maybe that is why there are some biblical texts that should be read and left alone. There is no need for commentary or for mounting a defense for someone to explain everything. It is enough with some texts simply to turn them loose in the room and allow them to do what they will.

This is the feeling I get when I read Paul in Romans 12. He introduces us into a world of experiences and values about which we don't talk very much, at least not directly. It is not because the world of the scripture is not our world. It is a world that appears to be a world of victims. Or at least a world of contradiction in that the Bible brings us things that do not seem to be the way to victory. The world that Paul brings us into is one of pain, joy, hope, and despair. When one reads the words of Romans 12, it seems a bit out of place. It doesn't sound like victory at all. It sounds a bit like a weakness to bless those who persecute and to weep with those who weep.

That's our world — we don't talk directly of these things not because we are cowards, but because we don't talk about some things because they are not supposed to be talked about. Some things in our relationship to God and to each other are strengthened in our silence. Our relationship is stronger and healthier when it is assumed, but when it is talked about, it dies, not because it's false, but because it is over-exposed. The house of faith has other rooms besides the den. There are times to sit on the floor and talk about everything that will come up. However, when you look around this house, there are other rooms, not so much for privacy but for intimacy. I simply cannot talk about everything in public, and somethings are better assumed.

Paul talks about things that do not relate well in our society. One is to repay no one evil for evil, but take thought for what is noble in the sight of all. This is to travel a way that is different from all others. "The Road Not Taken" was written by Robert Frost almost as a parody. It was written to poke fun at a man who had a hard time making decisions. It was only when Frost shared his poem with other poets that he realized this whole idea of making those hard decisions of life was no laughing matter. Paul, like the traveler in Frost's poem, must make some hard decisions.

Two roads diverged in a wood, and I —
I took the one less traveled by,
And that has made all the difference.

When life is lived on the other side of Paul's advice, it is a way of getting by without those hard decisions. It reminds me of the opposite of the Frost poem — one of those one-liners that could only come from Yogi Berra. "When you come to the fork in the road, take it." That statement brings a smile to the face, for it is futile. The road less taken is one that appears to be the road of a victim. At times, not only in this passage but also in the teaching of Jesus, that is the case.

I sat in a courtroom just as an observer and listened to the case of a couple who were divorcing. The judge finally said, after listening to the pleas of both sides, "It appears to me that this woman is a victim. A victim of an abusive and unkind husband."

Thinking of the victim's mentality, it seems like we only become victims when we lose our dignity. Through the poverty and despair of some people's lives, it is hard to know how anyone could keep their dignity. In James Agee's wonderful book, *And Now Let Us Praise Famous Men*, he looks at life in the South through the Depression era, and how those who had nothing made their lives more than would seem possible. He tells a story of a black man who worked at a sawmill, whose job it was to keep the mules. He was treated about like the mules were treated. But part of his job was to blow the whistle four times a day. He would take out his dollar watch on a greasy shoestring and at 8 a.m., he would pull the chain to get the men working. At noon he would pull the chain again to stop the men for lunch, after lunch at 1 p.m. to put the men back to work, and finally at 5 p.m. to send the men home. Agee lets us see that pulling that chain four times a day allowed the man to sit at the head of his table with his family with dignity and command their respect.

Paul said one may be victimized, but there must be a refusal to be a victim. Maybe he talked a lot about victims because they came close to Paul. They heard in his voice — they saw in his face — they knew in his ministry — here was sympathy and understanding.

It could be that they also found him to be a victim: this one who knew what it was to have been beaten and driven out of town, to be cursed, to be lied about, to be mistreated, to be slapped, to be mocked, to be joked about, and to be accused of not really being an apostle. They knew Paul to be a victim. Maybe that's why Paul's letters were read — here is a kindred spirit. They felt a strong sense of identity with Paul.

Paul knew of defeats, and there are those who would define life as a series of defeats — by all the things we have not done, or by the bad things that have been done to us. Our glass is never half full, but always half empty. Nothing we have accomplished appears in any way significant when compared with what we have failed to accomplish. We allow our failures to add up to failure, and our losses to make us losers, our defeats to defeat us, and ourselves to be diminished by the wrong that we have done.

Reinhold Niebuhr once wrote:

> *Nothing that is worth doing can be achieved in a lifetime, therefore we must be saved by Hope. Nothing which is true or beautiful or good makes complete sense in any immediate context of history, therefore we must be saved by Faith. Nothing we do, however virtuous, can be accomplished alone, therefore we are saved by Love.*

Paul is not calling on the people that are now called Christian to be the doormat of the world. Even though we may feel like comedian George Gobel when he was a guest on *The Tonight Show* years ago. As another guest arrived on the set, George said, "Did you ever feel that the world is a tuxedo and you are a pair of brown shoes?" There is a lifting away from the idea that we are living as Christians to be victims.

I recall someone's idea of our imperfection as we come to God. They said that our life is like a line on a page and God is another line on the page. However, it may be instead that we are like a line on a page, but God certainly isn't the other line and just comes to cross our living on occasion. The concept of Paul is that God is the page and we most certainly are the line on the page.

Paul writes this powerful letter to the Roman Christians and to those who live in a world that is far from being Christian to encourage them to take control of every situation, and that control is to let God be God. Let the one who has the complete control take care of the things we cannot. As Paul says, "Vengeance is mine, I will repay, says the Lord. No, 'if your enemies are hungry, feed them; if they are thirsty, give them something to drink; for by doing this you will heap burning coals upon their heads.' Do not be overcome by evil, but overcome evil with good." We can be victors, but not according to the way the world thinks. It must be in the way that God thinks.

**Proper 18
Pentecost 16
Ordinary Time 23
Romans 13:8-14**

A Call To Love

Of all the words used throughout the world, the one that is used the most — or misused the most — is "love." Love is not merely a denial of self. It is caring for others, and seeking their welfare above and before self. We use the word "love" to describe a great variety of experiences: feelings of the heart, conditions of the mind, expressions of our will, and our own actions. It is, therefore, extremely difficult to understand when people say that they "love," what that really means. Furthermore, because "love" has a tendency to be an ambiguous word, it can also be a dangerous word.

When you see the word or hear the word *love*, what do you see? I see a couple in their twenties looking at a little face wrapped in a pink blanket for the first time. I see an old man as he sits with his wife of 52 years. She has Alzheimer's. He knows that she will never get any better. Yet he tenderly and lovingly holds her, even though she doesn't know who he is. I see a middle-aged man during the Depression come into the house in the evening with a milk bucket in his hand. He pours milk into all the glasses before he pours his own.

The love that Jesus talks about is a love for those for whom we have little or no affection. As I thought about the kind of love that motivates me, I was reminded of Jesus' teaching. "You shall love your neighbor as yourself. Love does no wrong to a neighbor. Therefore, love is the fulfilling of the law."

It is true, we can go through the motion of doing God's will and never really love. An old couple in the congregation had been together for years. She had been after him for a number of years to be baptized. When I saw him coming down the aisle, my immediate thought was, "Finally, he has given his heart to the Lord." He made his confession. I baptized him. Afterward, as he was putting his left sock on, I said, "I'm very happy for you." He response jolted my innards. "I hope she's happy. I wouldn't have done this if she had left me alone."

I remember Paul's words when he deals with a congregation who has either lost their vision of love or needs to be reminded of this concept again. He writes to remind them that love is really an obligation. The sentiments of Paul are in keeping with the commandment form we know from the Gospel tradition (Matthew 22:34-40; Mark 12:28-31; Luke 10:25-28). Paul puts love on a level of obligation. It is not an emotional tone that makes you compelled to go about loving. This is why the whole law is reduced to two commandments: "Love God with all your heart, mind, soul, and strength, and your neighbor as yourself."

The idea is that this kind of love cannot hurt your neighbor. That is why it is the answer to every commandment. Christian unity and compassion are built on the foundation of this love that Paul is intent on sharing with the church. Paul's words that lift the idea of love come from his other writings as well as from Romans. Especially in the classic section about love from 1 Corinthians 13, he explains what he means about love.

> *Love is patient and kind; love is not jealous or boastful; it is not arrogant or rude. Love does not insist on its own way; it is not irritable or resentful; it does not rejoice in wrong, but rejoices in the right. Love bears all things, believes all things, hopes all things, endures all things.*

Paul says you can express all this, but without love it really doesn't count. It would be like playing a game with a four-year-old, and the rules change at every turn, or if it doesn't go right, they just say, "Doesn't count! I wasn't ready." However, Paul helps me figure out what love looks like — or at least what some of the results are.

To love without restriction is a difficult thing to accomplish. To show patience and kindness is extremely difficult. C. S. Lewis told about having lunch with a minister, the minister's wife, and their two children who were home from college for the weekend. All through the meal the minister dismissed his children's comments and opinions. He was as Lewis said both caring and careless. It is sometimes difficult to remember that love is to express that kindness even to family members.

Paul reminds us that our love, our expression of kindness, goes beyond that which we no longer want or need. To many, love is taking broken toys to the fire station. Love is taking a sack of groceries to people we don't know. But genuine love is the kind of care that does for others without regard to what one will receive in return.

I have had occasion to witness this kind of love in action. It was a rainy spring day in North Georgia. A knock came on my office door, and a man who looked vaguely familiar stood there, and behind him was a young woman almost hiding. He told me that she had been standing in the rain and he didn't know what else to do with her. She came in and sat in a chair in my office. She sat with her knees up in her chest. As I started talking to her I found out she was living on the streets and doing whatever was necessary to survive. I asked her if she needed something to eat, and she said she already had cocaine and whiskey, and nothing else was necessary. As the day wore on, we knew she needed help, and the church arranged for her to be taken to a hospital for drug addiction. After the word got out, the calls came in from members wanting to help, to visit, to do whatever was necessary to show their love. It was once in ministry that I felt the church was being a church. Unfortunately, she left and we never saw her again, but the effort put out by that church made me know if she would have accepted our love, then she would have had it.

If we could come away from this passage with a greater awareness, it would be to know that when all is done in church or as people, the gift that is left is love. Love will make a church and people grow. Love is that commodity that is greater than any other commodity in the world. When the fabulously wealthy Aristotle

Onassis died, his wealthy friends gathered together after the funeral, and naturally the main subject of conversation was how much he had and who got it? One exchange went like this: "How much did he leave?" The answer came: "Everything: he left everything."

Of all gifts that we can give or leave to someone else, the greatest gift is our love. It is the greatest of all commands and the one thing that the world seeks, but has the most difficult time understanding or receiving. It is Paul's word that reminds us of our call to love, and it must be our response to answer that call.

**Proper 19
Pentecost 17
Ordinary Time 24
Romans 14:1-12**

Who Am I To Judge Another?

While I was still in seminary, I thought it would be good to go back to my roots and try to understand a little more about my past and myself. There were things that I faintly remembered from my childhood. There were, however, large chunks of the past that completely escaped my awareness. So I took a trip to Samantha, Alabama, to see my great aunt Sally Boone who was already in her seventies. I vividly remember the visit. The day as I remember it was hot; she had opened all the doors and windows to let in a little breeze. We sat on the sofa, and she showed me newspaper clippings of her husband who had played minor league baseball in the 1920s and 1930s, and to make real money during the Great Depression had sold bootleg whiskey. I sat and listened, for what seemed like hours, about my family, and drinking sweet tea poured over ice as only Southerners can do. As the day wore on, Aunt Sally got out of her chair and said, "Come on, you need to meet some more of your family." We took a ride that hot summer afternoon to the Boone Cemetery. I did meet more family, and she told me about every one of them. As we walked around the headstones, I kept her talking by just calling out a name here and there. I finally called out one name that made her stop her stroll.

She looked at me and, with a bit of a laugh, said, "I never had much use for him."

I knew the story was getting good, so the questions came a bit faster. "Why didn't you have much use for him?"

She said, "Well ... he was one of those people that enjoyed being against anything that other folks were for ... It didn't really matter what it was. He was just against anything good people were in support of."

"He died about ten years ago. He was the kind of guy that sat in judgment of everyone, and he was never close to anyone, even his own family. He was never pleased about anything — at home — or at church. In fact, he caused more confusion over nothing than anyone else I have ever known."

As I studied this text, I realized that there were probably people in Paul's church who would cause confusion over the fact that they needed to be difficult. They were always in church, but picky, picky, picky — all the time.

In the city of Ephesus and also in the grand city of Rome, the church met in homes of members. These house churches would have enough room for several members. The worship in these house churches varied from group to group. Some used Latin in their service and others used Greek. Some were casual in worship, while others were very formal. Even the order of worship varied. There were some that had come to expect Holy Communion during a specific point in the service. But, knowing human nature, there were some groups that shared the Lord's Supper before the preaching, and then there were some groups that had it at the end of the service.

But what bothered Paul was the way they picked at each other. Some of you still keep the Sabbath. The problem isn't that they observed the Sabbath, but that they picked on everybody who didn't. Some believed the Sabbath is holy; others believed that every day is holy. Some were groups of Christians who drank wine, and others thought it was wrong to drink wine.

In Paul's mind the issue wasn't drinking the wine, for he said, "If you drink wine, drink it to the Lord. And if you refrain from drinking wine, then give the Lord the glory."

Paul also dealt with the issue of meat that had been sacrificed at an idolatrous shrine. This meat had been taken from a shrine and then to the market. The question was: Should a Christian eat the meat or not? It had been dedicated at a shrine just a few hours earlier. Some believers just ate vegetables and condemned those who ate the meat. Paul came along and said, "Stop all the foolish judgment about the foods." He said, "If you think it is wrong to eat meats, then don't eat meats. But do not sit in judgment of others who are comfortable eating meats." Paul said, "Just stop picking at each other, and know that judgment does not belong to us."

I grew up in a tradition that would argue about whether it was all right to have meals in the church building. There were long discussions about the way you could worship God. Was it all right to have an organ to assist in worship or was the music to be unaccompanied? Paul stops for a moment to try to get good people to realize it is not for us to get other people or groups to fit into our pattern. In other words, Paul says, "Knock it off! Whatever you do — do it to praise God, not to judge someone else."

You know, it is possible to observe some wonderful Christian habits and then, sour the whole thing by picking on people who don't do it the way you do it.

A lady called me one day after our television broadcast on Sunday evening with a question. She asked about a reference I had made about a recent movie I had seen. She quickly pointed out that she did not think Christians should go to the movies. She seemed to get a great deal of pleasure telling other people that she did not go to the movies, and showing disapproval for those who did. In fact, she seemed to enjoy giving the minister a little jab because he would go to a movie theater.

Paul stops and says: "In whatever you do or don't do, let everything be to the praise of God." That is your practice.

Christ is able — fully able — to save people who are different from you. You are in no position to judge, because you don't know why people do the things they do.

They have a background that is different from yours.

Father Joseph David from St. George Catholic Church and I shared a table at a local basketball awards banquet. After the meal I went for some coffee, and turned to Father David to see if he would care for some coffee. He said, "I don't drink coffee." He went on to tell me that when he was a child his mother would put Caster Oil into the coffee for the children to drink. He said he couldn't even stand the aroma of coffee. I had no way to know that about him. You never know where a person has come from or where they have been. That is why Paul says stop judging, for everyone will give an account to God.

Paul understood that being judgmental does not go along with the Christian life. When you hear the gospel and respond to the gospel, it heightens your sensibilities and sensitivities. You care more about things.

The gospel going through your veins will change you, and Paul says, instead of picking on each other, let your heightened sensitivity and love be devoted to what really matters in the world.

**Proper 20
Pentecost 18
Ordinary Time 25
Philippians 1:21-30**

Living On The Edge

In 1971 Evel Knievel attempted to jump across Snake River on a rocket-powered motorcycle. That episode ended with him pulling the parachute and floating into the canyon. It was only one of his many daredevil events, which always put his life on the line. Over and over again he would tempt fate and death. He would take his motorcycle to extremely high speeds and attempt to jump buses, fountains, and anything else that could be jumped. His purpose was to put himself in the greatest risk, in order to make the most money. He has been a person who has lived on the edge most of his life.

A seasoned veteran of the FBI investigated the possibility of any spy rings within the U.S. and beyond. He had been trained for special missions and knew every in and out of the spying business. His record was clean. He had worked on some of the highest profile cases in U.S. history. He was committed to National Security. In addition, he lived a very common lifestyle. Yet, it was this same man who was apprehended for selling U.S. secrets to the Soviets. This double life, this excitement of living on the edge, had lasted more than fifteen years.

It is not surprising that there is a daredevil who would allow his body to be thrown into the air and broken by the falls. Nor is it surprising that a spy would face imprisonment or even death if caught by the authorities. It is not surprising that there are people who live on the edge, knowing the end may come at any time. What may be surprising, however, is the fact that Paul is one of those people who lived on the edge. He wrote most of his letters from the edge. He lets us feel the mist in our faces, the fog in our throats, and the curling of our toes over the edge of eternity. It is to one of those passages that we now give our attention.

Paul takes time in the passage before us to slide everything to the edge, to the Parousia of Christ. Paul, not one to become melancholy about death, seems to view it as a promotion. "To live is Christ; to die is gain." This proclamation by Paul led people to wonder why he would feel this way about something that is so dreaded by so many. How can Paul look death in the face and say, "I really haven't decided as yet if I am going to live and come to you, or die and be with the Lord"?

Paul is not worried about death because he views death from a different perspective. Paul understands that this world is not his home. He is a pilgrim, just passing through. Jesus himself is credited with a saying that is preserved on the wall of a mosque near Delhi. It reads, "Jesus said, 'The world is a bridge; pass over it, but do not build your dwelling there.'" It sounds very much like the old hymn that says, "... this world is not my home I am just passing through...." The idea of Paul living a pilgrim life should not be odd or unusual to us. He expresses this in his writings over and over again.

We encounter this sense of not really being at "home," this sense of being a pilgrim, every now and then. What we find, are people who long for a time in their life that was a better, a more peaceful time. There are those times, however, when we find people who do not feel at home in this world any longer.

I once served in a most unusual staff situation. I was the senior minister. I served with a youth minister, an education minister, and a retired minister. The retired minister lived in a nursing home. He was transported in a wheelchair to the church where he taught an adult Bible class. This man was remarkable. At 88 years old, he had lost the use of his legs, and most of his sight was gone. His mind, however, was as keen as it had been thirty years earlier. Over a period of three years, his health continued to deteriorate, and finally he was confined to his bed. As we visited together, he told me the most difficult challenge for him was to understand why he was still there. One day he said, "You know I feel like this is not my home anymore." He was ready to go and be with the Lord. He felt like Paul: "to die is gain."

The Negro spiritual reminded the slaves of their vision, and empowered them on their journey through the wilderness to their freedom. These hymns spoke of a pilgrimage, and of their true home.

> *Go down, Moses, way down to Egypt's land.*
> *Tell ole Pharaoh, "Let my people go!"*
> *The Lord told Moses what to do*
> *To lead the children of Israel through.*
> *"Let my people go!"*

They understood that living in a land that was not theirs made them pilgrims, and magnified the fact that we are all pilgrims. Living on the edge is really living a pilgrim life. It is knowing that there is something much bigger than this planet to look for.

I was visiting a minister friend of mine when he was asked, "Reverend, do you believe in heaven?"

He replied, "I not only believe in it, I am looking forward to it." He said, "I am looking for what is there but maybe more than that I am looking for what isn't there."

For a while I didn't understand what he was talking about. Now I know exactly what he was talking about. He was talking about living on the edge, and how the view of the afterlife can and does affect this life. Paul was convinced that this life was worth living if you live it for some purpose. That is why he said, "... to live is Christ." To contribute something worthwhile to society or to the world makes life worth living. Otherwise, it is just existing and going through one day very much the same way the other days have gone.

Paul knew that life was tentative at best. On another occasion as he wrote to Timothy, he put down these words: "I have fought the good fight ... I have kept the faith. Therefore, there is laid up for me a crown of righteousness which the Lord the righteous judge will give me in that day."

Maybe to view the next life is to live on the edge, as John put it in his dazzling description of the New Heaven and the New Earth. In the new creation there are no more seas, which represents evil. All the things that hurt and destroy will be taken away. In fact, as you look at the Apostle John's description of the New Heaven, there are too many things to look for. But most of all, he tells us what isn't there. There is no more pain, no more tears, no more death. If we start taking away the things that are painful, we would take away much of the life. I started to think what I would take away. Here are only a few things: I would never go to the supermarket and see a child's face on a milk carton — no more missing children. I would not go to the poorer part of town and see people existing in substandard housing — no more slums. I would not be able to read about a Mrs. Miller who had lost her son in the Vietnam war, and a couple years later a young man, neat and nicely dressed, appeared at her door. He told her that he had known her son and had his footlocker in storage. He told her the only problem was that it would take about $200 to get it to her. Almost frantically, she took money that she needed for other things to give him for the footlocker. She never saw him again, and he was arrested a month later for taking advantage of those who had lost sons and daughters in that war — no more con artists.

For Paul living on the edge was a better way of life, because it was a life of hope and vision. He was very much like Abraham who looked for a city, a house not made with hands, whose builder and maker are God. To live on the edge is to know that in that place every brook is a baptistery, every stone an altar, every star a chandelier, every person a brother or sister, every table the table of the Lord, and every song a hymn.

Paul lived on the edge, a life that is higher and brighter than any other life. For on the edge, you cannot only see the world you live in, but also you go to the mountain and see the new promised land.

The Apostle Paul wasn't the only one who knew the value of living on the edge. As Saint Peter says:

Blessed be the God and Father of our Lord, Jesus Christ. By his great mercy we have been born anew to a living hope through the resurrection of Jesus Christ from the dead, and to an inheritance which is imperishable, undefiled, and unfading, kept in heaven for you, who by God's power guarded through faith for salvation ready to be revealed in the last time.

Living on the edge is not a bad place to live.

**Proper 21
Pentecost 19
Ordinary Time 26
Philippians 2:1-13**

The Mind Of Christ

As we read the writings of the Apostle Paul, we begin to get a sense through the Spirit that we are given the privilege to overhear his heart and soul. Not only is he a dedicated disciple, but also a very confessional preacher. For Paul to stop and ask something from prison is not out of character for him. When Paul makes those personal requests, it is a red flag, signaling a time to pay close attention, for here is the heart of the matter. This is the key to understanding. Paul's statements of instruction are more than instructions. He will draw a line in the sand. Then he will dare you to step across it. These statements are more like a test or a final exam: "Having the same mind, and the same love, being of one accord, and of one mind."

About five years ago, in the Windy City, Chicago, a few friends and I were out looking for a good place to eat. Someone said Morialli's Italian Restaurant was the place to eat. There was one slight problem: I didn't know exactly how to get there. I was driving and talking to the couple in the back seat, and as I looked up, it became apparent that I had just gone through a traffic light that was red. I cautiously scanned the area for local officials, hoping that my mistake had gone unnoticed. I breathed a sigh of relief when I saw no blinking red lights and heard no sirens. We drove a couple more blocks and decided that we had no idea where the restaurant was located. Seeing a group of people waiting to get into a pub, I pulled over to the curb to ask directions. Being parked improperly, the next thing I knew was that blue and red lights were doing a dance in my rearview mirror. I watched as two of Chicago's finest approached my car. One stood at the back and the other slid down the side. I put my window down, expecting a request for my license, but instead it was a question. "Well, you ran a red light, and you double parked. Are there any other city ordinances you would like to break tonight?" I did not know what to say, for it was not a question. It was a test, a final exam, and she really was not looking for an answer.

I have discovered that there are many questions in life that are not questions but final exams. For instance:

Honestly, son, have you done everything you possibly can on your homework?

I understand that you are expecting me to stay with the children tonight while you play tennis?

Do you love me? I mean really love me?

There was an even deeper one of these from the passage in Philippians 2. The situation is this: Paul is in prison. He is trying to encourage the Christians at Philippi. He writes to express a strong commitment. Paul's desire for the believers there is that their commitment will grow and develop, and someday surpass his own commitment, that tireless and ever-zealous discipleship.

Paul begins this section of the letter with some rapid-fire statements of loyalty and faith. Then he makes the heart of his argument, and it turns from being a statement of encouragement to a test. Paul did not want information, for he already knew the right answer: to have the same mind as he had in faith. All he wanted was for the believers to respond with and by faith. It was not a question; it was a final exam. Paul wanted self-disclosures on the part of the Philippians. It was almost as if he were saying, "It is easy enough to sit around and theorize what discipleship looks like. But we are called to be in the world." And here the world comes knocking on the door of the church, rapping on the window of the day care center, or a telephone call in the middle of the night — the teenager who is now pregnant; the hypodermic needles found in the parking lot; the man who sleeps in the breezeway of the church. The real world is coming and the question is: "Are we really disciples of Jesus Christ? Are we willing to give what it takes to show our love?"

What do you think the response should have been? What do you think we should say? Well, it seems to be a multiple choice test.

They could have given answer A, and maybe that is the answer Paul wanted. Answer A is the answer of those discerning disciples. This is the answer of people who know it is their obligation to roll up their sleeves in the face of human need and be ambassadors of reconciliation. These disciples understand that discipleship cannot be done in the abstract, but knee-deep in the murk and mire of human experience. This must be the answer Paul wants: "Lord, we will do it all." We do not know how. We do know, however, that Jesus gave his life for us, and with him all things are possible.

These disciples, if they were discerning disciples, knew that answer A was not the answer, for even the most dedicated disciple would not assume to be all that Jesus Christ was and is. I recall being on the board of the CPE program and one of the students saying, "I hate this job." We all asked, "Why?" She said, "There is so much human pain I cannot touch."

While I served a church in Calhoun, Georgia, I stopped by Mrs. Inez' home one morning. We sat and visited then she asked, "What will you be doing today?" I said, "Well, I need to run to Rome and visit the hospital." She paused for a moment, then said, "You must go by and see an old friend of mine. She is very sick and lonely." That afternoon after I did the visits on my list, I turned my attention to the note Mrs. Inez had written for me. The woman's name and room number were printed clearly on the card. I stopped by, and a small sign on her door read 'no visitors' so I immediately checked with the desk nurse. The nurse promptly inquired and came out saying the woman would like to see me. I opened the door into a dimly lit room and there was an elderly woman sitting up in bed with pillows to support what little weight she had. As I approached the end of the bed, she said, "So, you are a preacher?"

"Yes, Ma'am," and I told her my church affiliation.

With almost a glare she said, "Tell me who Lot's wife was."

I stood there a moment thinking, trying to remember the story of Lot and his family. I said without thinking, "The pillar of salt."

Her eyes brightened and she smiled. She said, "Sit down. I don't have a preacher."

We visited a bit and then as I departed I asked her permission to have prayer with her, and she agreed as someone who wanted but did not want payer. I asked if I could visit again, and she said she would like that. A few days later I went by again. This time the notice on the door was different, and there were flowers and a small welcome on the sign. The room was much brighter. We visited and I told her I would come again. Only two days had passed and now the sign had changed again. The sign had been removed from the door. I again inquired at the desk, and the nurse checked, but this time the answer was, "She said she will see you, but only you." Later that day Mrs. Inez called and said her friend had passed away. I think I did some good ministry with that woman, but she should have had more. She should have had the support of friends, family, and church, and not just a preacher she knew very little about. It cannot be answer A "Lord, we will do it."

So it must be answer B. This is the answer of the theologically discerning disciples. "Paul, how can we have the mind that our Lord Jesus Christ has? He is, after all, the savior of the world. And, it is presumptuous to think we can do anything with the human need in the world. Paul, your request has surely brought us to our knees. Paul, you are an apostle and, Jesus, you are the Lord. How can we be the disciples you need? I am not so sure."

There is something wrong with this answer too. It is the response of being a passive person, saying, "Be warmed and filled, for God will take care of you, but as for us, Sunday school is at 10 a.m. and worship is at 11 a.m." The mind of Christ brings us back to the reality of such a large task.

A few weeks ago, as I sat with a family in the hospital, I met a woman whose daughter had been in the hospital for three weeks. The problem was cancer. She asked me if I would visit her. When I went in, she sat up in the bed and thanked me for coming. She said, "I sing in the choir, but none of my church family has come to see me. They think it is something I did, so all they did was send me a card." There must be something more than "be warmed and filled" that is keeping us out of it.

Paul knew something that other disciples needed to know. He knew that God could use him in prison or on the seashore and he could take the meager resources and transform them into a strength and power. The mind of Christ, the transforming power of God, is still available to us as well as we go forth to do calls, or hospital visits, or hospice, or whatever it is that we are called to do as disciples of Jesus.

I attended a gathering of a spiritual renewal group. One night a successful businessperson spoke. Accompanying him was his family. His speech began to center on his family. He told about his spouse and three sons, and then told about his daughter. He said it was a surprise when they found out his wife was expecting. Then when she was born, they could tell by the characteristics that she had Down Syndrome. He told about the struggles they had early on knowing that their daughter would not have a life as they would have planned. Then he said something that seemed surprising. "She is the best thing that has come into our family." He then called his daughter up and as she hugged him, with tears in his eyes, he said, "She has the mind of Christ."

He could not fix the problem, but he could love, honor, and treat her with respect. It was obvious they had what thousands of other relationships did not have, and that was the presence of God. He used this scripture to talk about the way God used his heart and mind to love, help, and spread the news about God's goodness.

Yes, he said with his heart full of the morsels of mercy, "She has the mind of Christ."

Lectionary Preaching After Pentecost

The following index will aid the user of this book in matching the correct Sunday with the appropriate text during Pentecost. All texts in this book are from the series for the Second Reading, Revised Common Lectionary. (Note that the ELCA division of Lutheranism is now following the Revised Common Lectionary.) The Lutheran designations indicate days comparable to Sundays on which Revised Common Lectionary Propers or Ordinary Time designations are used.

(Fixed dates do not pertain to Lutheran Lectionary)

Fixed Date Lectionaries *Revised Common (including ELCA)* *and Roman Catholic*	Lutheran Lectionary *Lutheran*
The Day of Pentecost	The Day of Pentecost
The Holy Trinity	The Holy Trinity
May 29-June 4 — Proper 4, Ordinary Time 9	Pentecost 2
June 5-11 — Proper 5, Ordinary Time 10	Pentecost 3
June 12-18 — Proper 6, Ordinary Time 11	Pentecost 4
June 19-25 — Proper 7, Ordinary Time 12	Pentecost 5
June 26-July 2 — Proper 8, Ordinary Time 13	Pentecost 6
July 3-9 — Proper 9, Ordinary Time 14	Pentecost 7
July 10-16 — Proper 10, Ordinary Time 15	Pentecost 8
July 17-23 — Proper 11, Ordinary Time 16	Pentecost 9
July 24-30 — Proper 12, Ordinary Time 17	Pentecost 10
July 31-Aug. 6 — Proper 13, Ordinary Time 18	Pentecost 11
Aug. 7-13 — Proper 14, Ordinary Time 19	Pentecost 12
Aug. 14-20 — Proper 15, Ordinary Time 20	Pentecost 13
Aug. 21-27 — Proper 16, Ordinary Time 21	Pentecost 14
Aug. 28-Sept. 3 — Proper 17, Ordinary Time 22	Pentecost 15
Sept. 4-10 — Proper 18, Ordinary Time 23	Pentecost 16
Sept. 11-17 — Proper 19, Ordinary Time 24	Pentecost 17
Sept. 18-24 — Proper 20, Ordinary Time 25	Pentecost 18

Sept. 25-Oct. 1 — Proper 21, Ordinary Time 26	Pentecost 19
Oct. 2-8 — Proper 22, Ordinary Time 27	Pentecost 20
Oct. 9-15 — Proper 23, Ordinary Time 28	Pentecost 21
Oct. 16-22 — Proper 24, Ordinary Time 29	Pentecost 22
Oct. 23-29 — Proper 25, Ordinary Time 30	Pentecost 23
Oct. 30-Nov. 5 — Proper 26, Ordinary Time 31	Pentecost 24
Nov. 6-12 — Proper 27, Ordinary Time 32	Pentecost 25
Nov. 13-19 — Proper 28, Ordinary Time 33	Pentecost 26
	Pentecost 27
Nov. 20-26 — Christ the King	Christ the King

Reformation Day (or last Sunday in October) is October 31 (Revised Common, Lutheran)

All Saints' Day (or first Sunday in November) is November 1 (Revised Common, Lutheran, Roman Catholic)

Books In This Cycle A Series

GOSPEL SET
It's News To Me! Messages Of Hope For Those Who Haven't Heard
Sermons For Advent/Christmas/Epiphany
Linda Schiphorst McCoy

Tears Of Sadness, Tears Of Gladness
Sermons For Lent/Easter
Albert G. Butzer, III

Pentecost Fire: Preaching Community In Seasons Of Change
Sermons For Sundays After Pentecost (First Third)
Schuyler Rhodes

Questions Of Faith
Sermons For Sundays After Pentecost (Middle Third)
Marilyn Saure Breckenridge

The Home Stretch: Matthew's Vision Of Servanthood In The End-Time
Sermons For Sundays After Pentecost (Last Third)
Mary Sue Dehmlow Dreier

FIRST LESSON SET
Long Time Coming!
Sermons For Advent/Christmas/Epiphany
Stephen M. Crotts

Restoring The Future
Sermons For Lent/Easter
Robert J. Elder

Formed By A Dream
Sermons For Sundays After Pentecost (First Third)
Kristin Borsgard Wee

Living On One Day's Rations
Sermons For Sundays After Pentecost (Middle Third)
Douglas B. Bailey

Let's Get Committed
Sermons For Sundays After Pentecost (Last Third)
Derl G. Keefer

SECOND LESSON SET
Holy E-Mail
Sermons For Advent/Christmas/Epiphany
Dallas A. Brauninger

Access To High Hope
Sermons For Lent/Easter
Harry N. Huxhold

Acting On The Absurd
Sermons For Sundays After Pentecost (First Third)
Gary L. Carver

A Call To Love
Sermons For Sundays After Pentecost (Middle Third)
Tom M. Garrison

Distinctively Different
Sermons For Sundays After Pentecost (Last Third)
Gary L. Carver